Seeing Jesus
in His Own Words

Marianna Mayer

Phyllis Fogelman Books New York

This book is dedicated to
Jesus' teachings of compassion and forgiveness
for both friend and foe alike

Published by Phyllis Fogelman Books
An imprint of Penguin Putnam Inc.
345 Hudson Street
New York, New York 10014
Copyright © 2002 by Marianna Mayer
All rights reserved
Designed by Marianna Mayer and Nancy R. Leo-Kelly
Text set in Della Robbia, Sabon, and Koch Antiqua
Printed in Hong Kong on acid-free paper
10 9 8 7 6 5 4 3 2 1

Library of Congress Cataloging-in-Publication Data
Mayer, Marianna.
Seeing Jesus in His own words/Marianna Mayer.
p.   cm.
Includes bibliographical references.
ISBN 0-8037-2742-9
1. Jesus Christ—Words. I. Title.
BT306 .M39 2002   232.9'54—dc21   2001050145

Front jacket: Jacopo il Vecchio (c.1480–1523) *The Savior.*
Back jacket: August Andreas Jerndorff (1846–1906) *Jesus the Comforter.*
Title page: Gillis Congnet (fl.1640–1) *Christ Amongst the Birds and Bees.*

ART CREDITS:
Art Resource: pages 22 (Giraudon), 26 (Réunion des Musées Nationaux).
Bridgeman Art Library: title page (Phillips Fine Art Auctioneers, Scotland), pages 18–19 (Phillips Fine Art Auctioneers, Scotland).
SuperStock: front jacket, back jacket, pages 4 (Brooklyn Museum, New York), 6 (Brooklyn Museum, New York), 7, 8, 9 (Armenian Museum, Venice, Italy), 10–11, 12–13 (Christie's Images), 14 (Howard Rose), 15 (Musée des Beaux-Arts, Dijon, France), 16, 17, 20 (Musée du Louvre, Paris/ET Archive, London, England), 21 (Hermitage Museum, St. Petersburg, Russia), 23 (Johnny Van Haeften Gallery, London, England/Bridgeman Art Library/SuperStock), 24–25, 27 (Pinacoteca di Brera, Milan, Italy/Mauro Magliani), 28 (Christie's Images), 29 (Musée du Louvre, Paris, France/Lauros-Giraudon, Paris, France), 30 (Julia Condon), 31 (Keble College, Oxford, England), 32.

SOURCES: *The Acts of Jesus: The Search for the Authentic Deeds of Jesus*, Robert W. Funk and the Jesus Seminar, Polebridge Press, HarperSanFrancisco, © 1998. *All the Teachings of Jesus*, Herbert Lockyer, Castle Books, © 1997. *The Complete Gospels, Annotated Scholars Version*, edited by Robert J. Miller, Polebridge Press, HarperSanFrancisco, © 1992. *Cruden's Unabridged Concordance to the Old and New Testaments and the Apocrypha*, Alexander Cruden, Fleming H. Revell Co., © 1962. *The Holy Bible, New International Version*, International Bible Society, Zondervan Bible Publishers, © 1973, 1978, 1984. *The Holy Bible Red Letter Edition*, King James Version. *The Illustrated Guide to the Bible*, J. R. Porter, Oxford University Press, © 1995. *The Jerusalem Bible*, Doubleday & Co., © 1966. *Jesus Christ*, J. R. Porter, Oxford University Press, © 1999. *The Meaning of Jesus: Two Visions*, Marcus J. Borg and N. T. Wright, HarperSanFrancisco, © 2000. *Meeting Jesus Again for the First Time*, Marcus J. Borg, HarperSanFranciso, © 1994. *Nelson's Illustrated Encyclopedia of the Bible*, edited by John Drane, Thomas Nelson, Inc., © 1998. *The New Covenant, The New Testament*, Thomas Nelson & Sons, © 1946. *The New Revised Standard Version Bible*, published by the Division of Christian Education of the National Council of the Churches of Christ in the USA, © 1989. *The Revised English Bible*, Oxford University Press and Cambridge University Press, © 1989.

Seeing Jesus
in His Own Words

Jesus was guided into the wilderness and there he fasted. After forty days and nights Satan came to tempt him, saying, "If you are the son of God, change these rocks into bread."

And Jesus answered:

"It is written, that man shall not live by bread alone, but by every word of God."

Matthew 4:4; Luke 4:4

James J. Tissot (1836–1902) *Jesus Tempted in the Wilderness*

For some two thousand years Jesus' life and teachings have inspired people the world over regardless of religious tradition. Over that same time artists throughout history have been moved to create some of the most beautiful paintings based on his words and life.

To read his words is to recognize his great humanity and his godliness, for his words are simple and yet sublime, forever offering new and deeper meaning. This Man of Love so divinely above us and yet so completely approachable had an insight so unique, a personality so strong as to teach us the true attitude toward love.

With the fire of compassion Jesus instructs us in gentleness, humility, childlike wonder and innocence, forgiveness and generosity toward stranger, friend, and foe. This book sets out to demonstrate Jesus' character and teachings through a selection of his own words drawn from gospel narratives, combined with paintings by some of the many artists who were inspired to illustrate Jesus' profound spiritual wisdom and enlightenment.

In the gospels Jesus tells us that he will comfort all those who are in need:

"Come to me all you who are weary and burdened, and I will give you rest. Take my yoke upon you and learn from me, for I am gentle and humble in heart, and you will find rest for your soul. For my yoke is easy and my burden light."

Matthew 11:28–30

James J. Tissot (1836–1902)
Our Lord, Jesus Christ

August Andreas Jerndorff (1846–1906) *Jesus the Comforter*

And when he spoke of the power of his words, he said:

"*Everyone who listens to these words of mine and acts on them will be like the wise man who built his house on rock; and the rain came down, floods rose, gales blew and beat against that house, but it did not fall, because it had been well built . . . it had been built on rock.*

"*And everyone who hears these words of mine and does not act on them will be like the foolish man who built his house on sand. The rain came down, floods rose, gales blew and beat against that house, and it fell, and its fall was great.*"

Matthew 7:24–27; Luke 6:47–48

James J. Tissot (1836–1902)
Christ Goes to the Mountain to Pray

I. Aywasovski (1817–1900)
Chaos (The Creation)

8

During the day, Jesus was in the temple teaching, but he would sometimes spend the night on a hill called the Mount of Olives. And even on that hill the people from far and wide gathered to listen to his words.

This is what he told them:

"Blessed are the poor in spirit:
for Heaven's domain belongs to them.
Blessed are those who grieve:
for they will be comforted.
Blessed are the gentle:
for they shall inherit the earth.
Blessed are those who hunger
   and thirst for justice:
for they will feast.
Blessed are the merciful:
for they will receive mercy.
Blessed are those who are pure of heart:
for they will see God.
Blessed are those who work for peace:
for they will be known as
   the children of God.
Blessed are those who suffer persecution
   for the sake of justice:
for Heaven's domain belongs to them."

Matthew 5:1–10

Hendrick Krock (1677–1738) *Sermon on the Mount*

When the Pharisees saw that Jesus mingled and even dined with those they considered sinners, reviled tax collectors, and other outcasts, they were shocked. So they questioned his disciples, saying, "Why does your teacher associate with such people?"

But Jesus overheard them, and answered:

"*Since when do the able-bodied need a doctor? It's the sick who do. Go and learn what this means: 'It's mercy I desire instead of sacrifice. After all, I did not come to enlist religious people to change their ways, but sinners, for it is they who need me!'*"

Matthew 9:12–13; Mark 2:17; Luke 5:32

Christian W. E. Dietrich (1712–1774) *Christ Preaching in the Temple*

In the gospels Jesus described himself as a shepherd, and compared his followers to his flock. He said:

"I am the good shepherd; the good shepherd lays down his life for his sheep. I know my own and my own know me, just as the Father knows me and I know the Father; and I lay down my life for my sheep. And there are other sheep I have that are not of this fold, and I must lead these too. They too will listen to my voice, and there will be only one flock, one shepherd."

John 10:14–16

Jesus went on to explain that the good shepherd does not hesitate to leave his flock to go in search of the one lost lamb who has strayed. And just like the good shepherd, it is God's will that no one, however humble, shall be lost. Jesus said:

"There will be more rejoicing in Heaven over one repentant sinner than over ninety-nine virtuous souls who have no need to repent."

Luke 15:4–7

Margaret Winifred Tarrant
(1888–c.1959)
The Loving Shepherd

14

Philippe de Champagne
(1602–1674)
The Good Shepherd

There came a time when Jesus heard the disciples arguing over who among them would be the most worthy in the eyes of God. So he called them to him and questioned them. But immediately the disciples grew silent, for they were ashamed of what they had been saying.

And Jesus, knowing what was in their minds, said:

"In God's kingdom he who wants to be first must choose to be last. He, then, who wishes to be first in God's eyes must live humbly while on earth, and put the needs of others before his own."

Matthew 18

"If anyone wants to be first, he must make himself last of all and servant of all."

Mark 9:35

"For the least among you all, that is the one who is great."

Luke 9:48

It was about this time that a group of children ran to Jesus, and gathered around him. But his disciples began to chase them away. When Jesus saw this, he said:

"These are my children. All children must be free to come to me when they wish, for the kingdom of Heaven belongs to all who are as innocent as they.

"Look at this little one," he said, as he sat one child upon his knee. *"Unless you are as open and trusting as this child, you will have no chance of entering Heaven."* Finally he stretched out his arms and, gathering all the children to him, he blessed them.

Luke 18.15–17, Matthew 19:13–15; Mark 10:13–16

Francisco Pacheco (1564–1654)
Christ Blessing the Children

Hugo Vogel (1855–1920)
Jesus and the Children

The disciples asked: "Who will be chosen as the greatest in the kingdom of Heaven?"

In answer Jesus called a little child to him, and said:

"Truly I tell you, unless you change and become like children, you will never enter the kingdom of Heaven. Whoever becomes humble like this little child is the greatest in the kingdom of Heaven. Whoever welcomes such a child in my name welcomes me."

Matthew 18:1–5

George William Joy (1844–1925) *Christ and the Little Child*

Lorenzo Lotto (1480–1556) *Christ and the Adulterous Woman*

Peter asked Jesus: "Lord, if another sins against me, how often should I forgive . . . as many as seven times?"

And Jesus answered:

"Not seven times, I tell you, seventy-seven times."

Matthew 18:21–22

"And when you stand praying, if you hold anything against anyone, forgive him."

Mark 11:25–26

"You who listen, I say love your enemies, do favors for those who hate you, bless those who curse you, pray for your abusers."

Luke 6:27–28

And of standing in judgment over others, Jesus said:

"Don't pass judgment, so you won't be judged. Don't forget, the judgment you hand out will be the judgment you get back. And the standard you apply will be the standard applied to you."

Matthew 7:1–2

"Be as compassionate as your Father is. Don't pass judgment, and you won't be judged; don't condemn, and you won't be condemned; forgive, and you'll be forgiven."

Luke 6:36–37

"He that is without sin among you, let him be the first to cast a stone."

John 8:1–7

Rembrandt Harmensz van Rijn (1606–1669)
Return of the Prodigal Son

When Jesus spoke of generosity toward others, he gave this example:

"If someone presses you into service for one mile, go with him two. Give to anyone who asks; and do not turn your back . . ."

Matthew 5:41–42

"Treat people the way you want them to treat you."

Luke 6:31

". . . love your enemies and do good, and lend expecting nothing in return. Your reward will be great, and you'll be children of the Most High."

Luke 6:35

Hoping to test Jesus, a scholar standing amidst the crowd asked, "Of all the command-ments, which is the greatest?"

And Jesus answered:

"You are to love the Lord your God with all your heart and all your soul and all your mind. This commandment is first and foremost. And the second is like it: You are to love your neigh-bor as yourself. On these two commandments hangs everything in the Law and the Prophets."

Matthew 22:37–40

Leonardo da Vinci (1452–1519)
Head of the Saviour

Hans Bol (1534–1593) *The Good Samaritan*

While discussing compassion and generosity, Jesus added:

"You know, we once were told: 'You are to love your neighbor' and 'You are to hate your enemy.' But I say: Love your enemies and pray for your persecutors. You'll then become children of your Father in Heaven."

Matthew 5:43–45

"If you love only those who love you, what reward can you expect? There must be no limit to your goodness, as your heavenly Father's goodness knows no bounds."

Matthew 5:46–48

"Give to everyone who begs from you; and when someone takes your things, don't ask for them to be returned."

Luke 6:30

"Give, and it will be given to you."

Luke 6:38

"Be careful not to parade your religion before others; if you do, no reward awaits you with your Father in Heaven.

"So, when you give, do not announce it with flourish of trumpets, as the hypocrites do in synagogues and in the streets to win the praise of others. Truly I tell you: They have their reward already. But when you give, do not let your left hand know what your right is doing; your good deed must be secret, and your Father who sees what is done in secret will reward you."

Matthew 6:1–4

Karl Julius Milde (1803–1875) *The Merciful Samaritan*

Quentin Metsys (c.1466–1530) *The Moneylender and His Wife*

All those who might be tempted to put material goods above spiritual riches, would do well to remember these words of Jesus:

"For what will profit them if they gain the whole world but forfeit their life?"

Matthew 16:26–27

"Do not store up for yourself treasures on earth, where moth and rust destroy, and thieves break in and steal; but store up treasure in Heaven, where neither moth or rust destroy, and thieves break in and steal. For where your treasure is, there will your heart be also."

Matthew 6:19–21

Mattia Preti (1613–1699) *Saint Peter Pays the Tribute Money*

Eloise Harriet Stannard (1829–1914) *Spring*

When his followers worried about how they would manage in their daily life, Jesus reassured them, saying:

"Don't fret about your life—what you are going to eat and drink, what you are going to wear. There is more to living than food and clothing, isn't there? Look at the birds of the sky: They don't plant or harvest, or gather into barns. Yet your heavenly Father feeds them. Can any of you add one hour to life by fretting about it? Why worry about clothes? Notice how the wild lilies grow: They don't slave and they don't spin. Yet let me tell you, even Solomon at the height of his glory was never decked out like one of them."

Matthew 6:25–29

"So do not be anxious about tomorrow; tomorrow will look after itself. Each day has troubles enough of its own."

Matthew 6:34

Jean-François Millet (1814–1875) *The Angelus (After Restoration)*

And Jesus gave courage and strength to his followers, saying:

"I am the light of the world; anyone who follows me will not be walking in the dark, but will have the light of life."

John 8:12

"I am the door; by me if any man enter in, he shall be saved."

John 10:9

"I stand at the door and knock: If any man hears my voice, and opens the door, I will come in to him."

Revelation 3:20

Julia Condon (1997) *Flame Emerging from Water*

William Holman Hunt
(1827–1910)
Jesus, Light of the World

"I give you a new commandment: Love one another; just as I have loved you, you also must love one another. By this love you have for one another, everyone will know that you are my disciples."

John 13:34–35

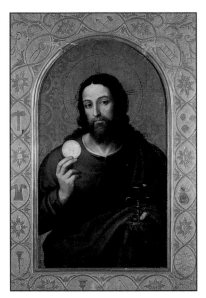

Juan de Juanes (c.1523–1579) *Christ with the Host*

About the Book

It is within the Gospels that we find Jesus' recorded words, and it is by his words that we come to know him more fully. Jesus himself tells us ". . . the mouth gives voice to what the heart is full of" (Luke 6:45). Indeed Jesus' message came directly from his being, natural and wise, proof of his goodness and godliness. The sampling of quotes presented in this book attempts to reflect Jesus' universal teaching of love for the innocent, the poor, the sick, the weak, for friend and enemy alike.

People of many traditions have long esteemed the sayings of Jesus as a powerful source of spiritual wisdom and enlightenment. In biblical times the reaction to Jesus was widespread, perhaps due in part to the fact that his method of teaching was direct and easy to understand. His words worked on the listener, going straight to the heart, transfiguring the lives of so many.

The disciple Paul describes the early Christian movement that followed the teachings of Jesus: "In Christ there is neither Jew nor Gentile, slave nor free male or female" (Gal. 3:28). Certainly no other great teacher has spoken more eloquently of compassion, generosity, forgiveness, and humility. His is a timeless social vision that continues to have striking implications for our lives today.